The Powhatan People

by Kim Covert

Consultant:
Chief Roy Crazy Horse
Powhatan Renape Nation

Bridgestone Books
an imprint of Capstone Press
Mankato, Minnesota

Bridgestone Books are published by Capstone Press
818 North Willow Street, Mankato, Minnesota 56001
http://www.capstone-press.com

Library of Congress Cataloging-in-Publication Data
Covert, Kim.
     The Powhatan people/by Kim Covert.
     p. cm. — (Native peoples)
     Includes bibliographical references and index.
     Summary: Provides an overview of the past and present lives of the Powhatan people,
covering their daily activities, customs, family life, religion, government, and history.
     ISBN 0-7368-0078-6
     1. Powhatan Indians—Juvenile literature. [1. Powhatan Indians. 2. Indians of North
America—Virginia.] I. Title. II. Series.
E99.P85C68 1999
975'.004973—dc21
                                                           98-7269
                                                              CIP
                                                              AC

Editorial Credits
Timothy W. Larson, editor; Timothy Halldin, cover designer and illustrator;
   Sheri Gosewisch, photo researcher

Photo Credits
Art Resource/Bruce Anspach, 18
Corbis/Grant Smith, 16
Jamestown-Yorktown Foundation, 8
Powhatan Renape Nation, cover, 6, 14, 20
Stockmontage, Inc., 10
Unicorn Stock Photos/Jeff Greenberg, 12

Table of Contents

Map

Canada

United States

Mexico

Traditional Location

Fast Facts

These facts tell how the Powhatan people lived many years ago. But the Powhatan people have changed as North America has changed. Today, the Powhatan live much like other North Americans. Many Powhatan people also value the ways of the past.

Homes: The Powhatan lived in rectangle-shaped homes with rounded roofs. They built the frames of their homes with wood poles. They made the roofs with sheets of tree bark. The Powhatan sealed the roofs with grass.

Food: The Powhatan were farmers and hunters. They ate vegetables from their gardens. The Powhatan gathered and ate fruits and nuts. They also ate meat and fish.

Clothing: The Powhatan wore clothing they made from leather. The clothing kept them cool during summer and warm during winter.

Language: The Powhatan language is part of the Algonquian language family.

Traditional Location: The central East Coast is the traditional Powhatan location. The Powhatan lived between what are now Virginia and New Jersey. Today, many Powhatan still live in this area.

The Powhatan People

Long ago, thousands of Native Americans lived in North America. The Native Americans had their own villages and languages. They also had their own ways of life.

Many Native Americans lived in what is now the United States. Some of these people lived on the central East Coast. They lived between what are now Virginia and New Jersey.

These people lived in groups. The people named their groups after the areas in which they lived. Some of these groups were the Mattaponi, Potomac, and Rappahannock.

These groups united under one government during the 1500s. They called the government the Powhatan Confederacy.

Today, many Powhatan people still live in their traditional homeland. Many live in Powhatan communities.

Today, many Powhatan people still live in their traditional homeland.

Homes, Food, and Clothing

The Powhatan people lived in comfortable homes. Traditional Powhatan homes were rectangle-shaped with rounded roofs.

Older Powhatan women were in charge of building homes. But everyone helped. They bent young trees to form the frames of their houses. The Powhatan covered the frames with layers of grass and bark. They made the roofs with sheets of bark.

The Powhatan were farmers and hunters. They ate vegetables women grew in gardens. The vegetables included corn, beans, and squash. The Powhatan also ate meat and fish.

The Powhatan people made clothes from leather. The clothing kept them warm in winter and cool in summer. Some of their clothing included leggings, skirts, and coats. The Powhatan also made shoes called moccasins.

The Powhatan people lived in comfortable homes. They wore clothes made from leather.

The Powhatan Family

Powhatan families lived in villages. Many family members lived together to share work and provide company. Parents, grandparents, and children lived together. Families also included aunts, uncles, and cousins.

Families always had a lot of work to do. Family members planted gardens. They built or fixed houses. Family members hunted and fished. They took care of young children. Family members taught older children Powhatan history and traditions.

Today, Powhatan families live like most other North American families. They own homes and live in communities. Parents work and children go to school.

Many Powhatan families live in communities on reservations. The Powhatan have saved these areas of land for themselves.

Powhatan families lived in villages.

Powhatan Spiritual Beliefs

The Powhatan people had their own set of spiritual beliefs. The Powhatan believed all life was sacred. They believed in showing respect for people and nature.

The Powhatan believed in giving thanks for all they received. They gave thanks for their families and good health. The Powhatan also gave thanks for the food nature provided.

The Powhatan people also had spiritual leaders. These leaders were good teachers. They taught children how to lead good lives. Spiritual leaders also helped people make hard decisions about right and wrong.

Today, many Powhatan people still follow traditional spiritual beliefs. Some Powhatan people combine these beliefs with other spiritual beliefs.

The Powhatan gave thanks for the food nature provided.

Powhatan Government

The Powhatan people have always had their own government. Each village chose men and women as leaders.

Communities met with their leaders to discuss important village business. Men, women, and children spoke at these meetings. Together, Powhatan community members made important decisions.

Leaders from each village also met as a group called a council. Each leader spoke for his or her village. The Powhatan council made decisions for the entire Powhatan Confederacy.

The English arrived in the 1600s. They settled on Powhatan lands. The English created their own governments. Powhatan leaders continued to meet as councils.

Today, Powhatan communities still have their own governments. Each community chooses a council and a chief as leaders.

Today, each Powhatan community chooses a council and a chief as leaders.

The Jamestown Colony

In 1607, English settlers arrived in Virginia. They asked the Powhatan people for permission to settle Powhatan lands.

The Powhatan agreed to share their lands with the English settlers. The settlers founded the Jamestown colony. A colony is a territory settled by people from another country.

The Powhatan helped the English settlers. They showed the settlers how to plant corn, beans, and squash. The Powhatan taught the English new ways to fish and hunt.

The settlers soon wanted the Powhatan to give up more land. The Powhatan people believed they had shared enough land. The English became angry. They fought the Powhatan. Many Powhatan people died.

By 1667, the English had taken the land they wanted. The Powhatan people had little land left. Many moved to other areas.

In 1607, English settlers asked permission to settle Powhatan lands.

Pocahontas

Chief Powhatan was an important Powhatan leader. He had a daughter named Matoaka. Matoaka was born in 1595. Powhatan people called her Pocahontas. This name means Playful One in the Powhatan language.

In 1612, the English took Pocahontas prisoner. They wanted Chief Powhatan to give them land for her return. Chief Powhatan would not. This made the English angry.

The English kept Pocahontas for more than one year. She then agreed to marry a settler to make the English happy. The settler's name was John Rolfe.

In 1614, Pocahontas married John Rolfe. John gave Pocahontas the name Rebecca. In 1616, John took Pocahontas to England. They stayed in England one year. Pocahontas died at the start of their trip back to Jamestown.

In 1612, the English took Pocahontas prisoner.

Public Powhatan Events

Today, the Powhatan people share their history and traditions with others. The Rankokus Reservation in New Jersey puts on a play about Pocahontas. The community also holds large events called festivals. The play and festivals are open to the public.

The Rankokus Reservation community acts out the Pocahontas play each August. The play is titled *The One Called Pocahontas*. It shows the life story of Pocahontas. This story is different from movies about Pocahontas. It shows what the Powhatan people remember about Pocahontas.

The Powhatan hold the American Indian Arts Festival each spring and fall. The festival features Native American art. Traditional clothing, storytelling, music, and dance also are part of the festival.

Traditional clothing is featured at the American Indian Arts Festival.

Hands on: Play Shinni

The Powhatan people play a game called shinni. The game is much like field hockey. The players use sticks and a small ball. They hit or kick the ball along the ground. They cannot touch the ball with their hands. They try to hit or kick the ball across a goal line. The goal lines are at the ends of a playing field. You can play shinni.

What You Need

An adult helper	A small ball
Strong cardboard	Four cones or other goal markers
Strong tape	Playing field or other large play area
Scissors	

What You Do

1. Ask an adult to help cut the cardboard into strips. Each strip should be 3 feet (1 meter) long and 6 inches (15 centimeters) wide. Lay the strips on top of each other to form a stick. Tape the stick together. Make a stick for each player.
2. Form two teams. Each team should have the same number of players.
3. Mark two goal lines with the cones. One goal line should be on each end of the playing field.
4. Try to hit or kick the ball across the other team's goal line.
5. Play for a set period of time such as 15 minutes. The team that scores the most goals wins.

Words to Know

confederacy (kuhn-FED-ur-uh-see)—a union of groups; Powhatan groups united under one government called the Powhatan Confederacy.
council (KOUN-suhl)—a group of leaders
festival (FESS-tuh-vuhl)—a large event that often is held at the same time each year
reservation (rez-ur-VAY-shuhn)—land that Native Americans have reserved for themselves
traditional (truh-DISH-uhn-uhl)—having to do with the ways of the past

Read More

Sita, Lisa. *Indians of the Northeast: Traditions, History, Legends, and Life.* Philadelphia: Courage Books, 1997.

Useful Address

Powhatan Renape Nation
Rankokus Indian Reservation
P.O. Box 225
Rancocas, NJ 08073

Internet Site

Powhatan Renape Nation
http://www.powhatan.org

Index